Gary Jones

Barcelona

First published by Gary Jones in 2016.

Copyright © Gary Jones, 2016.

All rights reserved. No part of this publication may be reproduced, stored, or transmitted in any form or by any means, electronic, mechanical, photocopying, recording, scanning, or otherwise without written permission from the publisher. It is illegal to copy this book, post it to a website, or distribute it by any others means without permission.

This book was professionally typeset on Reedsy.
Find out more at reedsy.com

Contents

Introduction	1
The Quirky Side of Barcelona	4
Transportation and Safety	9
Hotels	14
Getting to know Barcelona	17
Museums	29
Art Galleries in Barcelona	35
Where to Eat in Barcelona?	40
Coffee Shops	47
Bars	50
Barcelona's Festivals	54
Things that You Can Only Do in Barcelona	57
Conclusion	73

1

Introduction

This book was created for the short stay traveler. If you have limited time in Barcelona and want to experience the best the city has to offer, then this book will help you get the most out of your short stay.

Not many cities in the world have the atmosphere, and unique experience Barcelona has to offer. You will think of this amazing city long after you leave.

You will experience unique restaurants, strange museums, amazing bars, secret gardens and amazing tours.

Barcelona is a cosmopolitan city and in this great city you will experience elegance, harmony, and good manners. You will experience a world city and share public spaces with people from around the world that call Barcelona their home.

This cosmopolitan nature of Barcelona creates something special in the heart of Spain. The city is exciting and stimulating.

Thank you for downloading my book, and I hope you have an amazing time in Barcelona!

INTRODUCTION

Good Luck!

2

The Quirky Side of Barcelona

It is no secret that Barcelona was placed under the world's spotlight when it hosted the Olympics in 1992. The beginnings of its rise as one of the most popular tourist destinations in the world began at that moment. There were a lot of drastic changes made because of the said event.

National Geographic called Spain's second largest city as the Best Beach City of 1992. However, before the Olympic Games, the beaches of the city were literally overrun by factories and different industries. The city government actually had to move the businesses from the seashore and convert its entire 4.5 coastline into a beach and leisure area.

In effect, this piece of coast (and the rest of the city as well) was radically changed into the stuff that tourists adore today. If you're looking for a place that combines both the quirky and cool with the seriously gothic in one cup, then Barcelona will be quite a good pick.

What to Expect During your Visit
Many of the things you will find in and around Barcelona typically exhibit what you mostly will see in many European cities. You'll find

plenty of museums, churches, restaurants, outdoor markets, shops and many historic landmarks; but those are not the only things that make people want to come back – it's the city's cool character that usually draws in visitors in droves.

When to Visit Barcelona?

The quick and simple answer to this question is any time of the year is a good time to visit. Of course, the summer months starting in June are the most popular. People flock to the city's beaches to enjoy and relax.

However, the city is still bustling with life even during the off peak season. Do take note that many of the shops and some places of interest are closed starting in the month of August. The shop owners also need a break and they usually make the most of the off season by going on a much deserved vacation themselves.

Nevertheless, even in the cold autumn and winter months, tourists still flock to see the historic places here. They may not go to the beach during that time of the year but they visit the place for the appreciation of art and architecture. The serious side of the city is accentuated by the cold weather and the occasional rain.

BARCELONA

3

Transportation and Safety

The best way to get from the city is to take the RENFE train from the airport. The RENFE train service runs approximately every 30 minutes to and from Barcelona airport. The train will take you to the city centre. It takes about 25 min to get to the city. You can get off at Barcelona Sants, Passeig de Gràcia or Clot Stations. At these stations, you can connect to the Subway system.

Barcelona International Airport Website
http://www.aena-aeropuertos.es/en/barcelona-airport/index.html
Barcelona International Airport Map
https://goo.gl/maps/7YiUEnuGenn
Phone:+34 902 40 47 04

RENFE Website (airport train)

TRANSPORTATION AND SAFETY

http://www.renfe.com/EN/viajeros/

Metro Website
http://www.tmb.cat/en/home

The best way to get around the city is to use the subway. Barcelona has a world-class subway system. The subway is clean, safe and easy to use. Prices are reasonable, and various types of tickets can be purchased from vending machines.

The best ticket deal is to buy a city travel card that will give you access to the tram, metro and bus systems. This will cost around 5 euro. With these cards, you have unlimited use for the whole day.

Metro Website
http://www.tmb.cat/en/home

Travel Card Website
http://www.tmb.cat/en/barcelona-travel-card

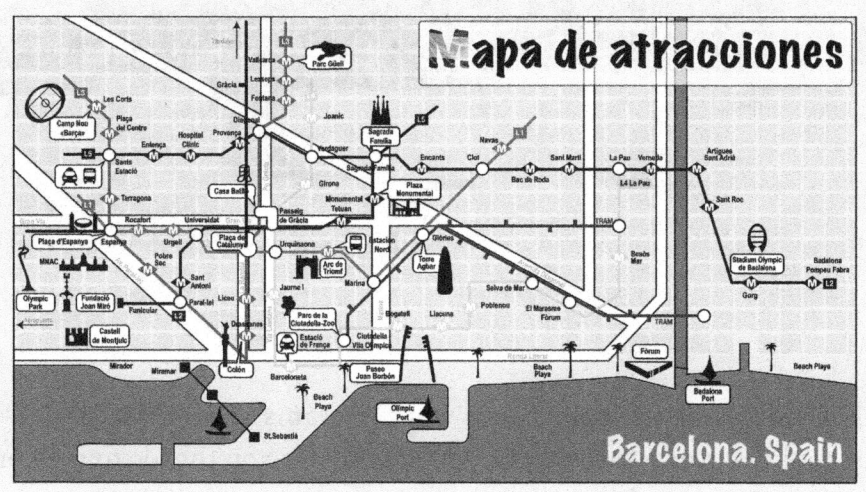

Safety

Barcelona is a safe city in general, however there are some problems with pickpocketing .Pickpocket criminals target tourists in places like subways or popular tourist spots.So be careful and make sure your valuables are in a safe place and not an easy target for a thief.

Be careful in the Ramblas.The Ramblas is the main promenade through the central part of the city.It is here that many pickpockets look for potential targets.So be careful.Its also a good idea to be very careful in this area at night and try to avoid it after 11pm.

These pickpockets sometimes work in teams and will try and use distractions to get you to lower your guard.So be on the lookout when strangers try to get too close to your personal space.It might be a setup to steal something from you.

It might be a good idea not to carry all your cash and credit cards in the same wallet. Leave some backup money at the hotel safe.

Have a great time in Barcelona, but be cautious.!

4

Hotels

We Boutique Hotel

The building where this lovely hotel is located was once home to the famous painter Josep Maria Sert.Josep Maria Sert was a friend of Salvador Dalí, the world renowned artist.The We Boutique Hotel is very elegant, and its location is great.The hotel only has six rooms, so it's nice and cosy with great service.

Address:2a, Ronda de Sant Pere, 70, Barcelona
Phone:+34 932 50 39 91
We Boutique Hotel Website
http://www.weboutiquehotel.com/
We Boutique Hotel Map
https://goo.gl/maps/vhdt78rAXWt

Casa Bella Gracia

This nice budget hotel is away from all the crowds of Barcelona and will give you a cosy hideout when visiting Barcelona.The location is in the village of Gracia and will give you a sense of being in traditional Barcelona with its small streets and fantastic atmosphere.Casa Bella Gracia is a modern hotel with a nice warm feeling to it.The hotel only has 12 rooms and has a lovely roof terrace for having a cup of coffee or breakfast.

Address:Carrer de Sant Agustí, 4, Barcelona
Phone:+34 638 49 34 28
Casa Bella Gracia Website
http://www.casabellagracia.com/en
Casa Bella Gracia Map
https://goo.gl/maps/g5Zh9zCb8J72

Praktik Bakery, Eixample Dreta

Praktik Bakery Hotel is a unique hotel concept in Barcelona where a hotel and bakery has teamed up.You have the rooms on the upper floors and the bakery on the ground floor.The rooms are not very big but it has everything you need and the great thing is you can just go downstairs and grab a coffee and fantastic fresh bread.

Address:Carrer de Provença, 279,Barcelona

Phone:+34 934 88 00 61
Praktik Bakery Hotel Website
http://www.hotelpraktikbakery.com/
Praktik Bakery Hotel Map
https://goo.gl/maps/9SdRwwxWLM92

Hotel Ciutat De Barcelona

Hotel Ciutat De Barcelona is located in the beautiful Born neighbourhood.This hotel is very basic but has great service and a very nice rooftop terrace with a pool.For a budget hotel, this is a very good deal and is located in one of the best neighborhoods in Barcelona.

Address: Carrer de la Princesa, 33 - 35, Barcelona
Phone:+34 932 69 74 75
Hotel Ciutat De Barcelona
http://www.ciutatbarcelona.com/
Hotel Ciutat De Barcelona
https://goo.gl/maps/D8gea8UU4FU2

Hotel Pulitzer

If you want to stay in a central location in Barcelona, and you don't mind the crowds, then this is good hotel for your stay.Although this area has a reputation for being a party area the hotel is fantastic and will give you a nice peaceful base away from the busy Barcelona streets.The hotel has a great design, and it has a very nice lobby with white leather sofas to take a break from your busy day in Barcelona.

Address: Carrer de Bergara, 8,Barcelona
Phone:+34 934 81 67 67
Hotel Pulitzer
http://www.hotelpulitzer.es/en/we/
Hotel Pulitzer
https://goo.gl/maps/v4H6KgGtY2u

5

Getting to know Barcelona

Las Ramblas

There is no doubt that when you visit Barcelona, one of the first things that will come to your mind is that it is a modern city. It's not completely modern, but it mixes some of the traditional with the new. You get to see that up close and personal in Las Ramblas.

There is usually a lot of traffic in this part of the city. Well, not exactly vehicular traffic. You only get foot traffic in this part of the woods. You can say that this is the most popular street (yes, it's a street) in Barcelona.

People sometimes call it La Rambla, note that that is a singular term. Well, that is also politically correct since it does look like just one long stretch of a boulevard. However, calling it Las Ramblas (the plural one) is also correct.

You see, it's not really just one street; it's five streets in a row. The name actually describes a stretch of five boulevards all lined up into a pretty long promenade. If you look hard enough (and if you have a map of the city), you can discover for yourself that the long boulevard starts with Placa Catalunya and it ends somewhere near the waterfront where the Columbus Statue is located.

Literally hundreds of people take a leisurely stroll on this two kilometer stretch of road. They enjoy the many historic landmarks along the way. They also get to try the many delicacies the city has to offer through the many shops lined up along the way.

You can do some souvenir shopping, enjoy some of the local color and watch street performers do their thing. Visitors can sit back and relax and enjoy some of that famous coffee that others have been raving about. It's a place where you can mingle with the people in what is arguably the most popular boulevard in all of Spain.

To get to Las Ramblas take the subway to Plaça de Catalunya Metro Station.

Las Ramblas Map
https://goo.gl/maps/UMYTJ9Py4Xt

Parc de la Ciutadella

Yes, this is a park, and it's also a historic place. Back in the day, this was once a fort; the name Ciutadella can be translated into "citadel." This is one of the most popular landmarks in the whole of lower Barcelona.

If you're a nature lover, then you will enjoy the pair of botanical gardens situated right here. Here, you will also find what people call La Cascada. These are two fountains designed by no other than the renowned architect Gaudi.

There is a lake where you can go rowing and enjoy the serene atmosphere. The huge statue of an elephant is also a nice place to take a selfie. Another attraction in Ciutadella is the Castell dels Tres

Dragons (literally Castle of Three Dragons) and a zoo. If you're visiting Barcelona and you have kids with you, then this is a good place you should not miss especially if you only have a couple of days to spare.

To get here take the subway to Ciutadella-Vila Olímpica Metro Station

Parc de la Ciutadella Map
https://goo.gl/maps/q1dCmzcbmRT2

Sagrada Familia

If you like visiting ancient churches and if you like to see architecture that you probably haven't seen before, then make it a point to stop by Sagrada Familia. Not only is this unique architectural marvel a thing that can make your breath stop, its design is also attributed to the now immortalized Antoni Gaudi.

A little tidbit of info here is the fact that Gaudi was not the original craftsman who was commissioned by royalty to oversee the construction of Sagrada Familia. It was originally given to Francisco de Paula del Villar, another famous architect.

Unfortunately, Villar wasn't able to complete the project since he was getting old. He retired in March 18, 1883 and the remainder of the work was given to Gaudi. The man then made a lot of drastic changes. These radical improvements were authentic and original. It's also one of the big reasons why the place is quite popular with tourists.

To get here take the subway to Sagrada Família Metro Station

Address: Carrer de Mallorca, 401, Barcelona
Phone:+34 932 08 04 14
Sagrada Família Website
http://www.sagradafamilia.org/
Sagrada Familia Map
https://goo.gl/maps/y47pfYMkMxu

La Ribera
Do you want to know how it feels like to live during medieval times? If that is the kind of thing you're into, then you're in luck. La Ribera offers just that. It is located on the western section of what is known as Ciutat Vella.

The name La Ribera can be literally translated into "the shore," which is basically where the place is situated. Go to the southernmost side of the place, and you'll find the sea right there.

Here, you will find a lot of traditional shops, which includes some weaver's shops (Carrer Cotoners), as well as rope making shops (Carrer Corders). Weavings and ropes aren't big industries nowadays, but they were important businesses in ancient times. Other than that, some of the more traditional shops you'll find here include mirror forgers and glazers.

Other than the entire section of medieval merchants (a great place to get some souvenirs you can brag about when you get home), you'll also find a lot of museums along the way. It's a great place to teach your kids some ancient European history. It's also a good way to appreciate life then and be thankful for the comforts of modern living.

To get here take the subway to Jaume I Metro Station

Address: Plaça Comercial, 11, Barcelona

Phone:+34 933 19 52 06
La Ribera Website
http://www.laribera.cat/
La Ribera Map
https://goo.gl/maps/kyKn3LCAsyk

La Placa de Catalunya

One way or another you will have to get to La Plaça de Catalunya. Well, this is the main transport hub of all of Barcelona. If you need to travel anywhere and you want to get a ride, then this is where you go to get one. Different forms of public transport can be found here – unless of course you prefer to travel on foot.

Since all the streets in Barcelona follow a rigid grid-like pattern, you will notice that all of the major routes will eventually lead here. It's like the hub of a wheel and all roads pass by this center. It's interesting that some people just call it "the square" (well if you look at a map, it will resemble some sort of a square right in the middle of the city).

This road and city design is the work of Ildefons Cerdà i Sunyer(Urban Planner) who was devising some sort of a utopian city plan. The way roads are designed, making extensions and expansions won't be a huge problem. The design also permits enough sunlight and ventilation to every city quarter. Now that is architecture with brilliant insight.

To get here take the subway to Plaça de Catalunya Metro Station

Address: Plaça de Catalunya,Barcelona
La Placa de Catalunya Map
https://goo.gl/maps/GzzpuKXpdyt

Tèxtil Café

Okay, so all that walking and all the medieval stuff can clog your memory so you ought to take a break, and one of the best places to do just that is Tèxtil Café. Here, you'll be enticed to order what the other people are having.

The seating is rather elegant no matter what time of the year it is. You can enjoy a light snack consisting of local pastries and a local brewed cup of coffee. The best part is that you're stretching your legs under the patio of a 14th-century mansion.

It's perfectly situated near two other famous landmarks, namely Museu Picasso (Picasso Museum) and Museu Tèxtil. Expect to meet other tourists and many locals here. You can enjoy the eclectic atmosphere and be on your way to continue on with your journey after a rather refreshing cup.

To get here take the subway to Jaume I Metro Station

Address: Carrer de Montcada, 12, Barcelona
Tèxtil Café Map
https://goo.gl/maps/dhvbitTbxe32

Marina Port Vell
Would you be interested in riding a yacht? You can actually book a day trip where you sail a classic yacht and travel along the city's coastline. It's a really adventurous and somewhat romantic thing to do. It's not anything like an extreme sport, but it's more of a relaxed and rather toned down way to enjoy the sea and the beautiful coast.

You won't believe it if one of the locals would tell you that Marina Port Vell didn't look as sublime a few years back. It was nothing but drab prior to 1992. Most of the place contained nothing more than piles upon piles of containers.

This was once part of the industrial zone. Nowadays, it has been transformed into a beautiful beach side with promenades along its path. This is also a great place to see some of the city's nightlife.

Here, you'll find the Moll d'Espanya with its famous but exclusive Club Marítim. You will have to make arrangements if you want to enter. However, making the extra effort will be worth your while.

There is also an IMAX cinema here where visitors can enjoy a movie together. If you're bringing kids along for the boat ride, they may want to visit the aquarium after you've had your lunch. There are also a lot of places of interest nearby.

Some of the other tourist attractions here include Reials Drassanes, which is the 14th century Royal Shipyards, the city's World Trade Center, the Moll de Barcelona, and the Torre de Jaume I.

To get here take the subway to Liceu Metro station.
Address: l'Escar, 26 (The Gallery Building), Carrer de l'Escar, Barcelona
Phone:+34 934 84 23 00
Marina Port Vell Website
http://www.oneoceanportvell.com/
Marina Port Vell Map
https://goo.gl/maps/8zt6RYRWTWP2

La Barceloneta and Port Olímpic

Have you ever wondered what the local street food tastes like? If you're a bit of an adventurer when it comes to tastes and flavors, then you might want to try the chiringuitos they sell here. Don't worry, they're safe to eat and won't upset your stomach.

They're basically just snacks and a lot of it should be seafood. This part of the city used to be an 18th century area where the working class lived. It used to be a downtrodden area but has since been transformed into a place where both locals and tourists can have a nice walk.

Another interesting thing that the locals do here is that this is where they walk their dogs. If you're looking for some of the best places to eat, then make it a point to visit this part of the city. You'll also spot some of the best nightlife the city has to offer.

To get here take the subway to Barceloneta Metro Station.

La Barceloneta Map
https://goo.gl/maps/hTpYkFrZJbA2

Address: Edificio de Capitanía, S/N,Barcelona
Phone:+34 932 25 92 20
Port Olímpic Website
http://www.portolimpic.es/presentacion.php?i=3
Port Olímpic Map
https://goo.gl/maps/uH5VdaHJTpL2

Santa María del Mar

Can't have enough of the old world architecture? Then see one of the city's finest in Santa María del Mar. It comes complete with stained glass windows, high steep vaults and the embrace of the nearby Mediterranean shore. That's a really picturesque view considering everything.

Some have said that this is one of the most well-preserved monuments that depict gothic architecture. The best part of it all is that you won't see the usual crowd gathering here. It's a great place to feel solemnity and be alone with your soul.

To get here take the subway to Jaume I Metro Station.

Address: Plaça de Santa Maria, 1, Barcelona
Phone:+34 933 10 23 90
Santa María del Mar Website
http://www.santamariadelmarbarcelona.org/home/
Santa María del Mar Map
https://goo.gl/maps/dG7oxqaLFXF2

6

Museums

Visiting a museum will transport you to various exciting times in history. It allows you to get to know your roots. It also allows you to enrich your knowledge about history.

Barcelona is a haven of many beautiful and rich museums. It is filled with fantastic and inspiring museums that will mesmerize you.

When you are in Barcelona, it is a must to visit the following museums:

Museu d' Historia de la Ciutat
This is THE city museum of Barcelona and it is for the ancient history buffs. You the entrance to this magnificent museum is through a beautiful 16th century mansion called Casa Padellas. Then you can walk past to the ancient Roman city of Barcino which is located in the underground levels of the museum. Here, you will discover the remains of the Placa Del Rei, a medieval royal palace.

Here are some of the places that you should visit when touring inside this museum:
- Roman funeral way
- Temple of Augustus
- Roman Domus of Saint Honorat

- Villa Joana
- Turo de la Rovira
- Outstaning Catalan Persons Gallery

Address:Plaça del Rei, s/n, Barcelona
Phone:+34 932 56 21 00
Museu d' Historia de la Ciutat Website
http://museuhistoria.bcn.cat/
Museu d' Historia de la Ciutat Map
https://goo.gl/maps/sQ5QqEPs3sB2

Museu Barbier-Mueller d'Art Pre-Colombi

This is a museum that is dedicated to pre-columbian art and cultures of South and Central America. You could find many precious South American jewelries in this museum. You will also find various statues, textiles, and ceramics.

Address:Carrer de Montcada, 14,Barcelona
Phone:+34 933 10 45 16
Museu Barbier-Mueller d'Art Pre-Colombi Website
http://www.barbier-mueller.ch/?lang=es
Museu Barbier-Mueller d'Art Pre-Colombi Map
https://goo.gl/maps/LBbHRmRFpn82

Museu de la Xocolata

If you love chocolate, then you should visit this museum. The Museu de la Xocolata is for kids and kids at heart. It is also for hard core chocoholics. This museum will allow you to trace the history of chocolate.

You can also find chocolate models of anythings from grand tourists attractions such as the La Sagrada Familia to beloved cartoon characters such as Sponge Bob, Tom and Jerry, and Winnie the Pooh. Kids will surely have fun inside "The Chocolate Museum".

Address:Carrer del Comerç, 36,Barcelona
Phone:+34 932 68 78 78
Museu de la Xocolata Website
http://www.museuxocolata.cat/?lang=en
Museu de la Xocolata Map
https://goo.gl/maps/7B7PfVJmSry

Museo del Perfume (Museum of Perfume)
Barcelona is a city full of special things to do.The Museum of perfume is one of the places that you have to visit.The museum has a wide variety of perfumes that date back to ancient times.This shop is a bit tricky to find because it's located at the back of a big perfume shop, but its worth a visit.

Address: Passeig de Gràcia, 39,Barcelona
Phone:+34 932 16 01 21
Museo del Perfume Website
http://www.museudelperfum.com/
Museo del Perfume Map
https://goo.gl/maps/3rUm5qfYqn92

Picasso Museum
There are not many people in the world that do not know who Picasso was.He is one of the greatest artists in History.This museum has one of the biggest collections of Picasso's work in the world.

There's no arguing about it, this is the most popular art museum in all of Barcelona. You put the name of Pablo Picasso on it and you should expect people to crowd around to appreciate the man's genius.

The Picasso Museum is located at the very heart of what is known as La Ribera.

It's surrounded by five old mansions that create an elegant old world atmosphere, which is quite rare nowadays. Even if you're not an art enthusiast, you will appreciate the collections they have on display here. The ones you'll find here are Picasso's more conventional works.

Picasso first set foot on this land way back in 1895. He arrived with his family. He immediately put up a studio, which was a pretty bold move at the time. The studio, if you're interested, can be found in Carrer de la Plata.

Here are some of the notable buildings that are occupied by the museum:
- Palau Aguilar – This is the first building that is occupied by the museum.
- Palau Meca – This palace has a beautiful central courtyard. It also has a polychrome coffered ceiling.
- Palau Finestres – This building was built in 1363 and it is currently used as an exhibition place.
- Casa Mauri – This building was acquired by Museu Picasso in 1999.

Address: Carrer Montcada, 15-23,Barcelona
Phone:+34 932 56 30 00
Picasso Museum Website
http://www.museupicasso.bcn.cat/
Picasso Museum Map
https://goo.gl/maps/fDUw9PqfTZx

National Art Museum of Catalonia Barcelona

This gallery focuses on Catalan visual art.The museum has a wide variety of artwork.There are different sections that focus on the Romanesque art, Gothic art, Renaissance art, Baroque art and Modern art.

Address: Palau Nacional, Parc de Montjuïc, s/n,Barcelona,
Phone:+34 936 22 03 60
National Art Museum of Catalonia Barcelona Website
http://museunacional.cat/en/getting-here
National Art Museum of Catalonia Barcelona Map
https://goo.gl/maps/VcoMKqSKzMm

Barcelona Museum of Contemporary Art
Your trip to Barcelona has to include a visit to this museum.The big collections that can be seen here is very special.The museum focuses on three periods,the 1940's - 1960's,1960's - 1970's,the last period is

contemporary.

Address: Plaça dels Àngels, 1, 08001 Barcelona
Phone:+34 934 12 08 10
Barcelona Museum of Contemporary Art Website
http://www.macba.cat/
Barcelona Museum of Contemporary Art Map
https://goo.gl/maps/nhghn4zxpk82

Museu Marítim

If you appreciate gothic art and architecture, then you will love what you will find in the Museu Marítim. It's near the Royal Shipyards, and it is a Naval Museum. You'll find here collections that testify of the glory of the old naval history of Barcelona.

One particular collection to note is the Great Adventure of the Sea. It's one of the more popular attractions here. It also includes miniatures of the ships that Ferdinand Magellan used to circumnavigate the world. As an ending note to the tour, you can get onboard one of the ships, the Santa Eulàlia, an ancient sailing ship that is currently sitting on the Moll de la Fusta.

Address:Av. de les Drassanes, s/n,Barcelona
Phone:+34 933 42 99 20
Museu Marítim Website
http://www.mmb.cat/
Museu Marítim Map
https://goo.gl/maps/DtUZUiqy2E92

7

Art Galleries in Barcelona

Aside from the museums, Barcelona also houses the most exquisite art galleries.

Here are some of the most interesting and art galleries in Barcelona:

Galeria Joan Prats
This is one of the pioneering art galleries in Barcelona. It was built and founded in 1976 and it is part of several popular art fairs like Arco and Art Basel in Miami Beach. It showcases contemporary art and it houses the work of various artists like Erck Beltran, Knut Asdam, Carla Zaccagnini, Carles Congost, and Hannah Collins.

Address:Balmes 54, 08007 Barcelona,
Phone:+34 932 16 02 90
Galeria Joan Prats Website
http://www.galeriajoanprats.com/
Galeria Joan Prats Map
https://goo.gl/maps/dGmqCg64mWz

Marlborough
Marlborough is one of the most popular art dealers in the word. It was

initially founded in London and it showcases the art work of artists like Francis Bacon, Henry Moore, Oskar Kokoschka, and Victor Pasmore.

>Address:Carrer d'Enric Granados, 68,Barcelona
>Phone:+34 934 67 44 54
>Marlborough Website
>http://www.galeriamarlborough.com/
>Marlborough Map
>https://goo.gl/maps/o7UJYhnxVvQ2

AB Galeria D'Art

The AB (Antoni Botey) Gallery of Art houses the fantastic work of both established and up-and-coming artists. This gallery showcases the work of Carles Vives, Vicenc Viaplana, Josep Ucles, Josep Maria Subirachs, Joan Ponc, Pablo Picasso, Marc Petit, Manolo Moreno, Ara Mikaelan, Josep Guinovart, Jaume Guinovart, Pere Galera, Margarita Escalas, Modest Cuixart, Jordi Cerda, Joaquim Camp, Josep Bofill, Erwing Bechtold, Eduard Arranz Bravo, and other established artists.

>Address:Carrer Agustí Vinyamata, 55,Granollers, Barcelona
>Phone:+34 938 70 73 52
>AB Galeria D'Art Website
>http://www.abgaleriadart.com/galeria/
>AB Galeria D'Art Map
>https://goo.gl/maps/99uvXY85cN72

Ambit Galeria D'Art

This gallery showcases contemporary art of established artists from Spain and from other parts of the world. This gallery showcases the art work of notable artists like Artur Heras, Fernando Cartes, Eaves Casamada, Xavier Franquesa, Perico Pastor, Josep Codina, Ignacio Bugos, JP Viladecans, Franco Monti, Carmen Garolera, Riccardo Licata, and Ramon Enrich.

Address: Carrer del Consell de Cent, 282, Barcelona
Phone: +34 934 88 18 00
Ambit Galeria D'Art Website
http://ambitgaleriaart.com/
Ambit Galeria D'Art Map
https://goo.gl/maps/AKiybRPFaCx

Artevistas Gallery

This hip gallery showcases the contemporary work of various artists like the following:

- Albert Blanchart
- Andrea Torres Balaguer
- Cane
- Chimera
- C. Llonch
- Asis Percales
- F. Diamond
- Laura Armato
- Gil Gelpi
- Irene Bou
- Gori Mora
- Lantonio
- Otero
- Peta
- Monika Gojer
- Marcel Rodriguez
- R. Elizegi
- Nuria Torres
- Nicolas Rico
- Kyle Bryant
- Zachari Logan
- Sergi Perez

- Pablo del Pozo
- Jey Alonzo

Address:Passatge del Crèdit, 4,Barcelona
Phone:+34 935 13 04 65
Artevistas Gallery Website
http://www.artevistas-gallery.com/en_GB
Artevistas Gallery Map
https://goo.gl/maps/TrAphvqujQr

Galeria A. Cortina

This gallery contains unique and beautiful modern and contemporary art. This art gallery was founded in 1981. This gallery showcases and deals the works of Miguel Barcelo, Francisco Bores, Maria Blanchard, Manolo Millares, Carlos Nadal, Albert Rafols Casamada, Pablo Picasso, Eduardo Chillida, Salvador Dali, Modest Cuixart, and many more.

Address:Carrer de València, 248,Barcelona
Phone:+34 934 87 68 86
Galeria A. Cortina Website
http://www.galeriacortina.com/
Galeria A. Cortina Map
https://goo.gl/maps/DEE5pGMGogA2

Agora 3 Galeria d'Art

This gallery features contemporary figurative artists of the 20th century. It showcases the work of Yolanda Martin, H. Tran, Joan Iriarte, Grau Santos, A. Alemany, T. Llacer, M.A. Soler, J. Balaguer, Nory Steiger, and J. Veciana.

This gallery is open from Tuesday to Saturday 11 am to 2 pm and 4 pm to 8 pm. It is also open on Sundays from 11 am to 2 pm.

Address:Carrer Nou, 20, 08870 Sitges, Barcelona
Phone:+34 938 94 03 38
Agora 3 Galeria d'Art Website
http://www.agora.es/
Agora 3 Galeria d'Art Map
https://goo.gl/maps/VRZibNLw1nS2

8

Where to Eat in Barcelona?

In Spain, all the items on the menu will be listed. Remember that you can't change anything on the menu, and you rarely can create your own courses (or add another course to your meals).

One important thing you should take note of is that most of the restaurants will be closed on 4 pm and will resume business at 8 pm. Shop and restaurant owners usually take siesta in the afternoon. In case you don't want to go hungry during the said times, better buy a snack you can carry with you.

However, there are international chains as well as other local restaurants that do accommodate tourists during siesta. If you find one along the way, then make a mental note (or better yet, write it down on your itinerary) of the place. In case you get hungry while visiting the different places in the city, then you can come back to the restaurant and have a full meal.

What Dishes do they Serve?

Don't fret if a lot of the dishes you'll be offered is no other than seafood. You're in the Mediterranean and so expect Mediterranean meals. Well, it does have a good mix of veggies and fruits so you are actually getting a healthy meal for your money.

You should, however, take note that the seafood here isn't particularly local. That's another setback when you convert an entire city to tourism. Among the items unique to the local cuisine are tapas that are usually sold in bars as well.

It's not a particularly healthy meaty helping, but it is definitely flavorful. Unfortunately, it's not cheap, so be prepared to pay extra for something that tastes great. Another thing you will also notice here is that many street stands sell waffles.

Most tourist guides won't tell you this, and you'll be left to discover this fact on your own. If you love waffles, you should try the ones sold here. They are a good striking contrast to the Belgian waffles that most people are used to eating. They smell great and they do taste just as good too.

So How Much Do I Pay for a Meal?

Food prices in any part of the world will tend to fluctuate. It doesn't matter whether you're in Barcelona or not. However, just to give you a rough estimate, a budget meal for one person in this city will cost something like 10 Euros. A mid-range meal for a single individual (which includes a drink) will cost up to 25 Euros. If you spend more money on food (above 25 Euros), then that is considered splurging.

Where to Find the Good Restaurants?

The really great restaurants can be found all over Barcelona. However, there are some places where you can find many clusters of food places, bars and restaurants where they serve scrumptious meals.

Barceloneta

One popular area even for the locals is known as Barceloneta. If you've become a fan of the local baked fish dish, then this is where you'll find some of its best versions. The dish is locally known as Paella. Another popular local dish is Arròs negre, which is a helping of black rice.

Barceloneta Map
https://goo.gl/maps/1tDgqLPhd4w

There are other sections of the city where you can find the good places to eat. That includes Eixample Esquerra, which is located between Gran Via and the famous Mallorca. Plaça Catalunya also has a good selection of restaurants you might want to try. Another good place to check out is El Born, which you will find right next to Barri Gòtic, another good place to sample the local cuisine.

- Eixample Esquerra
- Plaça Catalunya
- El Born
- Barri Gòtic

Restaurants
Can Costa

Since we have already mentioned Barceloneta, one particular place you might want to have your meal is Can Costa. If you love seafood, then this is where you might find your heart's delight. The place is located along Passeig de Joan de Borbón, which is pretty hard to miss.

If you find yourself lost, just look for the waterfront and then walk back one block and you'll see Can Costa right away. It's not really that hard to find. There is one important detail you should take note of; this is the place where the locals usually eat. This says everything you need to know about this restaurant.

If you relish in sampling the local cuisine, then try one of their highly recommended dishes, fideuà de paella. Yes, it's another baked fish dish but don't get disappointed. If you're dying for the genuine Catalan baked fish dish, then this is it. Notice, this dish doesn't incorporate rice – instead it has noodles!

If you can't have enough of the seafood served here, then make sure you order one of their baby calamaris. That's squid fried with breading. Remeber is that you should arrive here some time before 2 pm, or else you won't find a table. The place is quite popular, and there's no guarantee that you can reserve some seats.

   Address:Passeig de Joan de Borbó, 70
   Phone:+34 932 21 59 03
   Website
   http://www.restaurantecancosta.com/
   Can Costa Map
   https://goo.gl/maps/VVA9iw5JMLx

Bar Marsella

Another popular place to eat is Bar Marsella. It is located on Carrer Sant Pau 65. If you're looking for true blue Catalan meals, then this is another great place to get just that. You'll also appreciate the décor. Much of it is 19th century, which includes rafters, really classic heavy drapes and chandeliers hanging way up in the ceiling.

   To get here take the subway to Liceu Metro.
   Address:Carrer de Sant Pau, 65
   Phone:+34 934 42 72 63
   Bar Marsella Map
   https://goo.gl/maps/PgX43trLdvw

Set Portes

This is a classic old paella and seafood restaurant.This place has an amazing atmosphere and has been in Barcelona since 1836.The food here is amazing.

To get here take the subway to Metro Barceloneta.
Address:Passeig Isabel II, 14,
Phone:+34 933 19 30 33
Website
http://7portes.com/
Set Portes Map
https://goo.gl/maps/YhsoYyDvoCM2

Can Culleretes

Can Culleretes is one of the oldest restaurants in Spain and has ben around since 1786. Amazing food and great atmosphere. They serve a variety of traditional spanish dishes.

To get there take the subway to Metro Liceu.
Address:Carrer d'en Quintana, 5
Phone:+34 933 17 30 22
Website
http://www.culleretes.com/
Can Culleretes Map
https://goo.gl/maps/qQctvTnmpL12

9

Coffee Shops

Barcelona has many coffee shops and bars. If you are looking to have a relaxing time, it is best to stroll around the streets of Barcelona and discover the hip and classy coffee shops and bars in this magnificent city.

Here are some of the best coffee and pastry shops that you should visit while you are in Barcelona:

Café Salambo

This café is famous local landmark in Gracia. This is a perfect place to have cocktails and coffee with your friends. This café has a wide selection of cocktails like the Mexic (tequila, cream, and chilli), Roma (grappa and cream), and the Bombo (chocolate, condensed milk, and Cointreau).

Address:Carrer de Torrijos, 51
Phone:+34 932 18 69 66
Website
http://www.cafesalambo.com/
Café Salambo Map
https://goo.gl/maps/ALyrbN75rUG2

Cafes el Magnifico

This coffee shop has a tasting area where you can sample some of their delicious and well-prepared coffee drinks. You can also buy the best coffee beans in the world in this café. This coffee shop serves the best cappuccinos.

Address:Carrer de l'Argenteria, 64
Phone:+34 933 19 39 75
Website
http://www.cafeselmagnifico.com/
Cafes el Magnifico Map
https://goo.gl/maps/NGhjhLMMpHt

Cachitos

This cozy café has an elaborate and striking décor. But, it offers a great experience. Aside from coffee, this café serves a variety of dishes that are made of premium ingredients. This café also have good wines and cocktails.

Address:Rambla de Catalunya, 33
Phone:+34 932 15 27 18
Website
http://www.cachitosrambla.com/#inicio
Cachitos Map
https://goo.gl/maps/W57MjMFkhkC2

Caelum

This café has the best parties in Barcelona. They sell different kind of sweet treats that are made by nuns and monks in convents and monasteries all around Catalonia. This café also have a good selection of teas.

Address:Carrer de la Palla, 8
Phone:+34 933 02 69 93
Website
http://www.caelumbarcelona.com/
Caelum Map
https://goo.gl/maps/bgfMDENxvuz

Meson del Café

This place serves great coffee but you will be mesmerized by its ambience. This café and bar was founded in 1909. They serve great pastries and they serve delicious hot chocolate, too. This café will surely give you a different kind of experience.

Address:Carrer de la Llibreteria, 16
Phone:+34 933 15 07 54
Meson del Café Map
https://goo.gl/maps/js5kdUCmQKp

10

Bars

Here are the best bars that you should visit while you are in Barcelona:

Chill

Many young professionals love to visit this bar for coffee and drinks.Live DJ's and theme parties are hosted here.During the day Cafe Chill is a great place to meet for a cup of coffee.

Address:Carrer de Provença, 424
Phone:+34 934 76 22 70
Website
http://www.chillbarcelona.com/
Chill Map
https://goo.gl/maps/m8kf9opMXa52

L'Entresol

This bar is perfect for gin tonic lovers. This bar feels like a paradise. The decoration of this café is impressive. The place is painted with a great combination of red, white, and black colors. You can also find old picture frames on the wall. It also has great music selection. This bar plays funky, groove, and indie music.

Address:Carrer del Planeta, 39
Phone:+34 685 53 39 41
L'Entresol Map
https://goo.gl/maps/oA3uE653QVM2

Never Mind

This is a fun rock and roll bar with a 90's grunge theme.This place is a favorite with university students.The bar is great for a fun late night out with friends or alone.

>Address:Escudellers Blancs N°3 Bajos
>Phone:+34 678 55 01 52
>Website
>https://www.facebook.com/NevermindBcn
>Never Mind Map
>https://goo.gl/maps/6pYGPYP9pQH2

Xixbar

Barcelona locals love this bar so you have to visit it as well. This bar is an old dairy house that now serves the best tonics and gins in Barcelona. The tonics and gin served in this bar mixed with different ginger, cinnamon, mint, cucumber, and berries. This bar organizes several fun tasting events.

>Address:Carrer de Rocafort, 19
>Phone:+34 934 23 43 14
>Website
>http://www.xixbar.com/
>Xixbar Map
>https://goo.gl/maps/YLaRgsqA5jQ2

11

Barcelona's Festivals

Another reason why people visit Barcelona is their illustrious festivities. You can time your trip to the city and arrive just when one of these lively fiestas are on schedule. That way you get to witness everything first hand. Note that these fiestas are unique to Catalonia, which means you'll never even see them celebrated elsewhere in Spain.

Cavalcada de Reis

This is one of the very first festivities on schedule each year. It is celebrated on January 5th of each year. It's one of the festivities especially geared for children so you might want to bring your kids along for the trip. The highlight of this fiesta is the travel of the three wise men with lots of heavily decorated floats and street dancing.

Sónar

Are you a music lover? Then this is one of the festivities you shouldn't miss. The festivity doesn't only feature the local music. It also highlights advanced multimedia arts. It's not just for ancient and folk music, you'll enjoy the best music in the city as well.

Sant Jordi

Do you want to propose to the girl of your dreams? Do you want to make it during one of the most romantic events in the world? Then bring your girl to Barcelona during Sant Jordi. Don't forget the ring!

Walk around Barcelona during Sant Jordi and don't be surprised if the locals shower you with flowers. This is their equivalent of Valentine's Day. Take note that it is customary for men to give flowers to women and women give books to the men. Sant Jordi is celebrated on April 23 of each year.

Fira de Santa Llúcia

If you want to celebrate a different Christmas with your loved ones, then try spending the holiday season here in Barcelona. You'll get to witness Fira de Santa Llúcia. This festival is scheduled on December 13th of each year and the entire week leading to Christmas is usually festive. It's like having an entire week with the Christmas spirit in your heart.

Revetlla de Sant Joan

If you enjoy fireworks, then you will love Revetlla de Sant Joan. This fiesta celebrates the midsummer solstice and is quite festive. It is celebrated on June 23rd of each year, and fireworks usually light up the night sky 24/7. It's a night of festivities and a time to party the night away.

La Mercè

This feast is rather solemn and is celebrated on September 24th of every year. This is actually one of the oldest feasts in Barcelona. It dates all the way back to the 17th century. It features a lot of parades, music events, fireworks and magic fountain activities. The best part is that on the last night everyone gets to have all they want of Barcelona's local liquor known as Cava.

Now, these are only some of the many festivals that are held year round. Remember to schedule your trip carefully. Take note of the different places of interest and have a rowdy good time when you visit Barcelona.

12

Things that You Can Only Do in Barcelona

Traveling to Barcelona will give you great and exciting memories. Barcelona is a city like no other, and there are things that you can only do in Barcelona.

Here are some of the activities that you can do while you are in Barcelona:

(1) Have dinner and stroll on Las Ramblas

Las Ramblas is the main tourist destination in Barcelona. This 1.2-kilometer pedestrian stress is packed with souvenir shops, cafes, restaurants, hawkers, and street performers. Here are some of the major attractions in Las Ramblas:

Erotica Museum

Address:La Rambla, 96 bis
Phone:+34 933 18 98 65
Erotica Museum Map
https://goo.gl/maps/6QsEscL1dUH2

Barcelona Wax Museum
Address:Passatge de la Banca, 7
Phone:+34 933 17 26 49
Barcelona Wax Museum Map
https://goo.gl/maps/BhDSMB00Ks92

Modernist Boqueria Market
Address:La Rambla, 91
Phone:+34 933 18 25 84
Modernist Boqueria Market Map
https://goo.gl/maps/A6FM8vNQh5C2

Christopher Columbus Monument
Address:Plaça Portal de la pau, s/n
Phone:+34 932 85 38 32
Christopher Columbus Monument Map
https://goo.gl/maps/hw7JB0omQkJ2

White Painter Statue
Address:Passeig de Colom, s/n
White Painter Statue Map
https://goo.gl/maps/zKimT1gnn7s

You can also find the mosaic by Joan Miro within the promenade in Las Ramblas. You can find various flower shops where you can find unique and fresh flowers.

It is also a must to set aside a few hours to go around La Boquera.

This is one of the oldest market in Barcelona and in Spain. You can find a wide variety of fruits. It is also a must to buy the traditional sausages and chorizo. Also, don't forget to enjoy and beautiful stained glass and Art Nouveau architecture in the market.

(2) Ride the "Steel Donkey".

Of course, the term "steel donkey" is a euphemism for a bicycle. You can go on a bike tour in Barcelona. But, the Steel Donkey Bike tour is not your ordinary bike tour.

When you go on a Steel Donkey Bike Tour, you'll visit the charming back streets the village district of Gracia, the old industrial ruins of Poblenou, and the back streets of El Bourne. You can find many many flea markets, squat houses, and recycled workshops while you are on this bike tour.

Address:The Green Bike Shop, Carrer Ample 53
Phone:+34 657286854
Email: info@steeldonkeybiketours.com

Website
http://www.steeldonkeybiketours.com/
Steel Donkey Map
https://goo.gl/maps/hpYxQ3zPUsy

(3) Get Electric on A Bicycle
Aside from the standard Steel Donkey Bike tour, you can also go on an e-bike tour. It is a memorable experience where you get to have fun racing with city cars, too.

Address:Carrer de Montsió, 10
Phone:+34 902 02 77 20
Bicycle Website
http://www.barcelonaebikes.com/en/
E-bike Map
https://goo.gl/maps/v7j2MDBEoaJ2

(4) See Madonna on a Magic Hill
You can visit the image of Virgin Mary called Black Madonna in Barcelona. This statue is located at the Montserrat Abbey in the high peaks of Montserrat Mountain. Many pilgrims from all over the world go up in the high mountains to see this statue. But, many people travel to Montserrat Mountain for other reasons. This "jagged" mountain has a breathtaking view. You can also go on wine tour near the Montserrat mountain.

Phone:+34 938 77 77 77
Website
https://www.montserrat-tourist-guide.com/
Black Madonna Map
https://goo.gl/maps/Zvkj893xpt12

(5) Go on a Barcelona Booze Cruise

You can go on a Barcelona Booze Cruise and drink like a sailor! When you go on a Barcelona Booze Cruise, you will enjoy tasty barbeque, beer, sangria, and cocktails. You can also enjoy the music of resident DJs and games. The Barcelona Booze Cruise is definitely for party animals.

Phone:(+34)602 660 736
info@boozecruisebarcelona.com
Booze Cruise Website
http://www.boozecruisebarcelona.com/

(6) Drive a Ferrari Around an F1 Circuit

It is not every day that you get to drive a Ferrari and it is definitely not every day that you get to drive around the Circuit de Catalunya which is the official track of the Spanish F1 Grand Prix. Well, the good news is, you can do this in Barcelona. You can also pretend that you are James Bond while you are driving on the way to Monte Carl.

Address:Camino Mas Moreneta
Phone:938864451
Website
http://en.circuitcatexperience.com/
F1 Circuit Map
https://goo.gl/maps/57Pp9NudpG52

(7) Dine in a Dark Area

The famous Dance Le Noir? is not your ordinary restaurant. This restaurant will provide a great sensory experience because in here, you will eat your dinner in a lightless room. Most of the restaurant's waiters are blind. The food is great and if you want to try something different with your friends, you should have dinner in Dance Le Noir?. Dining in this restaurant is definitely a memorable experience.

Address:Passeig de Picasso, 10

Phone:+34 932 68 70 17
Website
http://barcelona.danslenoir.com/
Dance Le Noir Map
https://goo.gl/maps/7UbJnrxDte22

(8)Cover your body with chocolate!

Barcelona is a city of pleasure. It is a must to get a massage in Barcelona. You can experience different kinds of massage in this city. You can try the famous chocolate massage. This will allow you to experience what it feels like to get covered in chocolate! You can try the sea shell massage, too.

Address:Carrer de Mallorca, 180
Phone:+34 930 00 91 65
Website
http://kbcenters.com/
Map
https://goo.gl/maps/8uQhqqdW9B22

(9)Go on a Treasure Hunt

You can go on a treasure hunt while you are in Barcelona. This fun activity will allow you to explore the winding streets of Barri Gotic. If you win, you get a bottle of Spanish wine as a prize.

Address:Plaça dels Pirineus, 3-4
Phone:+34 932 80 92 74
info@bcn-adventure.com
Website
http://www.bcn-adventure.com/en/teambuilding/city-treasure-hunt.php
Map
https://goo.gl/maps/3DGRfr23T8C2

(10) Explore the Beautiful Park Guell

The Park Guell is a magical spot that is great for picnic. You could find various tourist attractions inside the park. You can find municipal garden inside the park. You can also find the Gaudi's beautiful mosaic salamander called "El Drac".

Here are some of the things that you should see while visiting the Park Guell:
- The Viaduct
- The Pavilion
- The Colonaded Pathway
- The Ceiling Mosaic in Hypostyle Room
- The Bird Nests

Phone:+34 902 20 03 02
Website
http://www.parkguell.cat/
Park Guell Map
https://goo.gl/maps/4NNxwYKRf3Q2

(11) Enjoy the Magic Fountain Show

This is a "must see" Barcelona attraction. You will never see a fountain like the Font Magica Fountain. This fountain was built in 1929. Around 2 million tourists visit this fountain every year.

Address:Plaça de Carles Buïgas, 1
Magic Fountain Map
https://goo.gl/maps/ZrK383JPT6J2

(12) Enjoy the Camp Nou Experience and FC Barcelona Museum

There is nothing like watching the Barca play a home match. But, you should also visit the FC Barcelona Museum. Camp Nou also has the largest Nike stores in the world. You can also buy affordable FCB scarves and T-shirts at stalls outside the stadium during match days.

Address:C. Aristides Maillol, 12
Phone:+34 902 18 99 00
Website
https://www.fcbarcelona.com
/tour/buy-tickets
Camp Nou Map
https://goo.gl/maps/6LmftNyVJKP2

(13)Discover unique and fantastic modernist buildings
You will discover many beautiful and awe-inspiring modernist buildings in Barcelona. When you are in Barcelona, you should go

and see these buildings:

Casa Amatler
Address:Passeig de Gràcia, 41
Phone:+34 932 16 01 75
Website
http://www.amatller.org/
Casa Amatler Map
https://goo.gl/maps/b3HGG8exMWK2

Casa Mila
Address:Provença, 261-265
Phone:+34 902 20 21 38
Website
https://www.lapedrera.com/ca/home
Casa Mila Map
https://goo.gl/maps/pbdty3Up8Vr

Casa Batillo
Address:Passeig de Gràcia, 43
Phone:+34 932 16 03 06
Website
https://www.casabatllo.es/
Casa Batillo Map
https://goo.gl/maps/5Q5bhuFPYk72

Casa Batillo is one of the most beautiful buildings in Spain. It was designed by the great Antoni Gaudi. In fact, it is one of his masterpieces. It is located at the heart of Barcelona.

Casa Mila is also a fascinating modernist building. It is also known as La Pedrera. It was designed by Josep Maria Jujol and Antoni Gaudi.

Casa Amatler is a unique, modernist building designed by Josep Puig Cadafalch. The design is a mix of Catalan and Flemish style.

(14) Tour inside the Sagrada Familia

There is nothing like the Sagrada Familia. It is one of the most unique and most recognized structures in the world. This magnificent church was constructed 1882 and it was designed by the world famous architect Antoni Gaudi.

You would be amazed by the remarkable geometric details. The church organ will also amaze you! It has 1,492 pipes!

Here are some of the architectural gems and monuments that you should see when touring inside this holy church:

- Nativity façade
- Nave ceiling
- The Sacred Family Cathedral
- The Glory Façade
- Museu Gaudi
- Apse
- The stained glasses
- The RosaryChapel
- The Passion Façade

Whether you are a devout Catholic or not, you will definitely enjoy the tour inside this magnificent church.

Address:Carrer de Mallorca, 401
Phone:+34 932 08 04 14
Website
http://www.sagradafamilia.org/
Sagrada Familia Map
https://goo.gl/maps/VPQ2dhdLz2N2

(15) Climb the Montjuic Hill
Climbing the Montjuic Hil will provide an awesome and unforgettable experience. You will find the Palau Nacional, the Magic Fountain, and the Mies van der Rohe Pavilion.

The Monthuic hill is also the home of the Anella Olimpica or the Olympic Ring. You can find the various sports facilities that are specially built for the 1992 Olympics.

If you are a nature lover, you will truly appreciate the beauty of the Montjuic gardens. You will be amazed by the beauty of the Montjuic botanical garden called Nou Jardi Botanic. If you are a cactus lover, you should also visit the Jardins de Mossen Costa I Llobera.

The oldest structure in the Montjuic hill is the Castell de Montjuic. It was originally built as a fortress to protect Barcelona from its enemies.

Montjuic Hill Map
https://goo.gl/maps/LtkL1Y2godD2

(16) Explore the mountain of Tibidabo

You could enjoy the beauty of Barcelona by climbing the mountain of Tibidabo. You could find the beautiful Sagrat Cor Church on top of this mountain.

You can also take a ride in the famous Red Aeroplane. This is a single carousel that will allow you to enjoy the view of the city.

Tibidabo was featured in the movie Vicky Cristina Barcelona. Tibidabo has a beautiful, scenic view that will take your breath away.

Barcelona is an wonderful city that you should visit during your lifetime. You could visit museums that highlight the city's rich culture, charming tourist spots, and do memorable things that you could not do anywhere else in the world.

Tibidabo Map
https://goo.gl/maps/8wj2z7KLNzR2

13

Conclusion

I want to thank you for reading this book! I sincerely hope that you received value from it . I hope you now have a better idea of what this amazing city has to offer.

If you received value from this book, I want to ask you for a favour. Would you be kind enough to leave a review for this book on Amazon?

Ó Copyright 2015 by Gary Jones - All rights reserved.

This document is geared towards providing exact and reliable information in regards to the topic and issue covered. The publication is sold with the idea that the publisher is not required to render accounting, officially permitted, or otherwise, qualified services. If advice is necessary, legal or professional, a practiced individual in the profession should be ordered.

- From a Declaration of Principles which was accepted and approved equally by a Committee of the American Bar Association and a Committee of Publishers and Associations.

In no way is it legal to reproduce, duplicate, or transmit any part of this document in either electronic means or in printed format. Recording of this publication is strictly prohibited and any storage of this document is not allowed unless with written permission from the publisher. All rights reserved.

The information provided herein is stated to be truthful and consistent, in that any liability, in terms of inattention or otherwise, by any usage or abuse of any policies, processes, or directions contained within is the solitary and utter responsibility of the recipient reader. Under no circumstances will any legal responsibility or blame be held against the publisher for any reparation, damages, or monetary loss due to the information herein, either directly or indirectly.

Respective authors own all copyrights not held by the publisher.

The information herein is offered for informational purposes solely, and is universal as so. The presentation of the information is without contract or any type of guarantee assurance.

The trademarks that are used are without any consent, and the publication of the trademark is without permission or backing by the trademark owner. All trademarks and brands within this book are for clarifying purposes only and are the owned by the owners themselves, not affiliated with this document.

http://shortstaytravel.com/

Made in United States
Orlando, FL
29 March 2025